the
Triumph of Eve
& Other Subversive Bible Tales

Teacher's Guide

Matt Biers-Ariel

The Complete Leader's Companion to The Triumph of Eve and Other Subversive Bible Tales by Matt Biers-Ariel

Walking Together, Finding the Way

SKYLIGHT PATHS®
PUBLISHING
Woodstock, Vermont

The Triumph of Eve & Other Subversive Bible Tales Teacher's Guide

2005 First Printing
© 2005 by Matt Biers-Ariel

ISBN 1-59473-152-7

10 9 8 7 6 5 4 3 2 1

Manufactured in the United States of America

SkyLight Paths Publishing is creating a place where people of different spiritual traditions come together for challenge and inspiration, a place where we can help each other understand the mystery that lies at the heart of our existence.

SkyLight Paths sees both believers and seekers as a community that increasingly transcends traditional boundaries of religion and denomination—people wanting to learn from each other, *walking together, finding the way.*

Walking Together, Finding the Way
Published by SkyLight Paths Publishing
A Division of LongHill Partners, Inc.
Sunset Farm Offices, Route 4, P.O. Box 237
Woodstock, VT 05091
Tel: (802) 457-4000   Fax: (802) 457-4004
www.skylightpaths.com

Contents

Introduction

How to Use This Guide

This teacher's guide is appropriate for all readers of *The Triumph of Eve and Other Subversive Bible Tales.* Younger students may be most attracted to the fun activities; adults will find questions that delve deeply into the stories' themes. This guide includes twelve lessons, one for each story. The lessons stand alone and don't build on prior lessons, so they can be taught in any order. Timing for lessons assumes a one-hour class. The lessons can be easily adjusted to meet different class lengths by adding or subtracting individual activities that have been provided for use with each story. All the lesson plans follow a similar format:

Themes for each lesson/story.

Opener to start each class with. Usually there will be more than one to choose from. Openers often include journal writing, in which case you should let students write on the topic for five to seven minutes and then facilitate a short class discussion. It is recommended that each student have a journal dedicated to this class.

Close Study of the Original Text, followed by guided discussion to gain deeper insights and ask questions that are sometimes glossed over in Bible classes.

Reading *The Triumph of Eve.* To use time efficiently for classes less than an hour in length, these stories can be read prior to class meetings. This section includes questions to facilitate class discussion.

Creative Activities allow students to personalize themes and stories.

Closure summarizes the lesson.

Sources are listed when appropriate.

Introductory Lesson

This is a thirty-minute lesson meant only for students who are unfamiliar with midrash. If students understand what midrash is, skip this lesson.

Theme

Introduction to midrash. The Hebrew term *midrash* literally means "probing" or "searching." Midrashim (plural) are stories that elaborate on Bible stories. Beginning with a close study of the original Bible text, the midrash often provides a moral lesson.

Opener

Write "What is midrash?" on the board. Discussion should help explain that midrash are stories about stories in the Bible.*

Close Study of the Original Text

There are two major reasons for writing midrashim.

1. To provide missing information.

    Ask students: According to Jewish tradition, who was the first Hebrew, the first person to discover monotheism? (Abraham)

    How old is Abraham when he is introduced in the Bible? (Seventy-five years old)

    What happened earlier in his life? (We don't know.) Explain to students that the

---

*Teacher might want to make distinction between Midrash and midrash that some traditional Jews make. Some Jews believe that Midrash with a capital *M* is a specific rabbinic literature that refers only to stories found in the Talmud and other ancient rabbinic writings. They believe that modern stories about the Bible should be referred to as midrash with a small *m,* or simply as "stories."

5

Bible usually tells stories very succinctly. Because of this, there is often a great deal of information missing from biblical stories, such as what Abraham did during the first seventy-five years of his life. If there was a specific unresolved issue in the Bible that the Rabbis needed an answer to, they wrote a midrash. For example, the Rabbis wanted to know how Abraham discovered monotheism.

Ask students to guess how Abraham discovered monotheism.

Read or summarize the midrash of Abraham discovering monotheism as a ten-day-old baby. This story—"The Babe Proclaims God"—can be found on page 189 of *Legends of the Jews: Volume I*, by Louis Ginsburg. Here is a quick summary of the midrash:

> Nimrod, the king, read in the stars that a boy would be born who would destroy paganism; therefore, all male babies were to be killed. A pregnant woman, Emtelai, gave birth in a cave outside of a city and returned home, leaving the baby by himself. The angel Gabriel provided milk for the baby to suck from the little finger of the baby's right hand. When he was ten days old, the baby walked out of the cave and gazed at the stars saying, "These are the gods." But when dawn came, he said, "These are no gods." The sun came up, and he said, "This is my god." But the sun set, and he said, "This is no god." The moon came up and he called her his god, but when a cloud covered the moon, the baby Abram said, "This, too, is no god. There is One who sets them all in motion."

2. To remedy confusing or conflicting Bible stories.

   Ask students: Who killed Goliath? (David)

   Read 1 Samuel 17:4–7, 48–51. Here it is David who killed Goliath.

   Then read 2 Samuel 21:19, the second account of Goliath's death. Here it is Elhanan who killed Goliath.

   Ask students to explain the contradictions.

Students should either write a midrash explaining the two different times Goliath is killed or explaining how Abraham discovered monotheism.

The Triumph of Eve

Teacher explains that they will be reading *The Triumph of Eve*, a book of twelve modern midrashim.
   Optional: Assign as homework the first story, "The Triumph of Eve."

The Triumph
of Eve

Themes

Mortality

Human purpose

Gender roles

Opener

Do one of the following journaling exercises.

Make a list of the pros and cons of immortality. If you could live forever, would you? Why or why not?

If you were to give our species a job, what would it be? Explain why you think this job is the most appropriate one for our species.

Close Study of the Original Text

Do the following activity.

Read excerpts of the Garden of Eden story: Genesis 2:4–9, 15–25, 3:1–19.

Each student should write down one question he or she would like to ask Adam, Eve, the serpent, and God.

Choose students to play the roles of Adam, Eve, the serpent, and God, and let them answer some of their classmates' questions.

Specific questions to consider, if they have not been asked:

- Why did God put the tree in the garden and then declare it off-limits?
- Why did Eve take the first bite, not Adam?

- What was Adam doing while Eve ate the fruit?

- Why did he take a bite when Eve offered the fruit to him?

- Do you think eating the fruit was the right thing to do?

- How do you think the world might have been different if Adam and Eve didn't eat the fruit?

Reading "The Triumph of Eve"

If the class has not already read the story, teacher should either read it out loud, put students in small groups to read it to each other, or allow fifteen minutes for students to read it silently. After the story has been read, invite discussion of the following questions.

How would you describe this story's version of God?

Do you think God could really be like this? Why or why not?

According to the story, God created humans in order to care for Creation. Compare this view to what you wrote in your journal at the start of the class.

This story changed the original biblical text by casting Eve as a heroine rather than as a villain. What do you think of this change?

One of the themes of the story is that mortality, or at least knowledge of our mortality, is essential to motivate our work on Earth. Do you agree?

Is there specific work you are striving to do in your lifetime?

If you knew you only had one year to live, would you live your life differently? Ask the same question for one month, one week, one day, one hour, one minute.

Creative Activities

Do one of the following activities.

1. Break students into groups of four or five. In fifteen minutes, students should prepare a skit that either:

   - Adds a new character to the story

   - Depicts the day after Adam and Eve ate the fruit

   - Explores the Garden of Eden story from any other midrashic perspective

   - Teacher may want to provide students with a bag of three or four props that must be used in the skit. Props can be random items such as a comb, a ball, or a shirt.

Each group should then perform their skit for the class.

2. Assign roles to four students. One should be Serpent, one Adam, one Eve, and one God. With the help of the other students, have them dramatize a one- or two-minute version of the original story or the *Triumph of Eve* version.

The students should perform their skit two times, so they know it well.

Have either the same group or four new actors perform the same skit, but in a different dramatic genre, such as horror, comedy, mystery, soap opera, or opera.

Closure

Each student volunteers one insight learned during the lesson. It can relate to the story, the student's own life, or the human species.

Cain's Co-Defendant

Themes

God's role in the world—deism versus theism

Dealing with anger

Opener

Do one of the following journaling exercises.

Do you believe that God intervenes in the world? Give an example or two to support your position. (During this discussion, explain the difference between deism and theism. A deist believes that God exists but does not get involved in the affairs of the world. A theist believes that God does get involved in the world.)

Have you ever been so angry at a person that you thought you'd like to kill him or her? Explain.

Close Study of the Original Text

The story of Cain and Abel (Genesis 4:1–16) is very short, so it is easy to read it all. After the story has been read, invite discussion of the following questions.

Do you think Cain had any justification to be angry and act out?

Did God's lack of intervention mean that God shared some of the responsibility for Abel's death?

Did God give Cain a fair and appropriate punishment?

It would be difficult to turn this story into a movie because it is so short. What scene(s) could be added in order to make a more complete story?

Reading "Cain's Co-Defendant"

If the class has not already read the story, teacher should either read it out loud, put students in small groups to read it to each other, or allow fifteen minutes for students to read it silently. After the story has been read, invite discussion of the following questions.

Was Cain justified in asserting that God was his co-defendant?

If you were God, would you intervene in the world today? If yes, where and how would you intervene? If no, why not?

If you do not believe that God intervenes in the world, how do you explain why most religions are filled with stories of God's interventions?

God was described in this story not as being perfect, but rather "a little rough around the edges." What do you think of this description?

Creative Activities

Do one of the following activities.

On a large piece of butcher paper, have students make a mural showing evidence of God acting in the world. If there are students who do not think God acts in the world, have them make a mural representing their beliefs.

Place the story in modern times and have students write the scene of Cain killing Abel. Students should consider props, setting, Cain's motivation, and God's role.

Closure

Each student offers a single word or phrase to describe God's role in the world.

Sources

Tanhuma, Bereshit 9; Genesis Rabbah 22:9, 12

Noah's Cracked Rainbow

Themes

The nature of humans

People's capacity to change

Reading the Bible as an adult, not a child

Opener

Do the following exercises.

Ask students: Which Bible story have you most often seen rendered as a children's book? (Noah and the Flood)

Have students write in their journals about what they think the story of Noah teaches.

When they're done, the group should discuss the answers they've come up with.

Close Study of the Original Text

Teacher explains that the Flood story does not end with the animals leaving the ark, God making the covenant, and everyone living happily ever after. The story continues with an episode between Noah and his son Ham. Read Genesis 9:18–29. After the story has been read, invite discussion of the following questions:

Why did Noah give Ham such a harsh punishment for simply seeing him naked? (Rabbis explain that uncovering one's nakedness is a euphemism for a sexual crime. The Rabbis argue that Ham did a sexually perverse act to Noah. That is the reason for the punishment.)

If Ham did something bad to Noah, then what is the lesson of the story? (Even though God tried to rid the world of evil, God failed. Evil is an inherent part of humanity.)

Do you agree that people have the tendency to do evil?

Reading "Noah's Cracked Rainbow"

If the class has not already read the story, teacher should either read it out loud, put students in small groups to read it to each other, or allow fifteen minutes for students to read it silently. After the story has been read, invite discussion of the following questions.

What is the significance of the title, "Noah's Cracked Rainbow"?

Noah knew that his fellow humans were headed for disaster, yet he was only concerned with saving himself. Was this justifiable?

What could Noah have done to change his neighbors' behavior? Do you think he would have been successful?

The story implies that while it is easy to see faults in others, it is difficult to see one's own faults. What is your opinion about this?

If the Flood didn't destroy the badness in the world because humans are inherently a mixture of both good and evil, did it serve any purpose? Did it teach humanity anything?

Gabriella thought that humans have too much power "for a bit of blood and bones." Do you agree? If so, how can human power be kept in check?

Creative Activities

Do one of the following activities.

Bring in lots of stuffed animals (ask students to do so, also) and have students create a puppet show: "A Day in the Life of the Ark."

Have two students create short dialogues revolving around the following situations. Each student should have two other students beside him or her. One of these students should portray the student's good inclination (in Hebrew, *yetzer ha-tov*), and the other the bad inclination (in Hebrew, *yetzer ha-ra*).

- A teacher suspects a student of plagiarizing an essay
- Two best friends both like the same boy, and the boy asked one of the friends out on a date
- A teen that is not part of the "in group" is offered alcohol at a party by someone who is part of the "in group"

Write a story about what God might believe to be evil in today's world.

Closure

After reading "Noah's Cracked Rainbow," do you still think the story of Noah should be a subject for children's books?

Sources

The Story of Raven comes from Genesis Rabbah 33:5. Ham's crime comes from Genesis Rabbah 36:4–5, and 7.

Reasonable Faith

Themes

Reason versus faith

The utility of sacrifice

Miracles

Hearing the voice of God

Opener

Do one of the following journaling exercises.

Is religious faith an answer to one or more of the moral issues facing the world, or is religious faith a problem in and of itself?

(Explain that since Sarah had gone through menopause, the birth of Isaac was a miraculous birth.) The Bible is filled with miracles. Make a list of biblical miracles. How do you define a miracle? Can you think of an example of a miracle in the modern world?

Close Study of the Original Text

Read Genesis 22:1–19. For many, the *Akedah* (the Binding of Isaac) is one of the most difficult texts in the entire Bible. After reading, the class creates a list of problems with the story. Discuss possible midrashic solutions to these problems. Questions to consider:

Abraham was well over one hundred years old at the time of the story. Presumably Isaac was stronger than his father, which is why he carried the wood on his back. How then was Abraham able to bind Isaac?

God was the one who directed Abraham to sacrifice his son, yet it was an angel who stopped Abraham from doing so. Do you think this is significant?

Abraham passed God's test of his faith, but did he have *too much* faith?

Do you think faith can be dangerous? How?

Reading "Reasonable Faith"

If the class has not already read the story, teacher should either read it out loud, put students in small groups to read it to each other, or allow fifteen minutes for students to read it silently. After the story has been read, invite discussion of the following questions.

While the idea of making a sacrifice in the form of a burnt offering is an ancient notion that has gone out of favor, many people do make religious sacrifices. Do you believe that there is merit in the act of sacrifice? What types of sacrifices might be appropriate in the modern world?

This story shows a balance between reason and faith. Do these concepts ever come into conflict in your life?

Abraham claimed at the end of the story that he heard the true voice of God. Have you ever heard the voice of God? How would one know if he or she was hearing the true voice of God or something else?

Creative Activities

Do one of the following activities.

Assign roles to three students. One should act as Abraham, one as Isaac, and one as an angel of God. With the help of the other students, have them re-create a one to two-minute version of Abraham's sacrifice of Isaac.

Perform the skit two times, so students know it well.

Have the same group, or three new actors, perform the same skit, but in a different dramatic genre, such as horror, comedy, mystery, soap opera, or opera.

Some midrashim claim that Abraham actually killed Isaac. In Christianity, some theologians see Isaac as representing Christ. Write a midrash that assumes Abraham killed Isaac.

Closure

The Binding of Isaac is one of the Torah readings for Rosh Ha-Shana, the Jewish New Year. It is a day for self-examination and commitment to growth and change of habits. Is this reading a good choice? Why or why not?

The
Trickster
Transformed

Themes

Finding God or the Divine Spirit

Revenge and forgiveness

Opener

Do one of the following journaling exercises.

Do you think there is a part of you that is immortal, such as your spirit or soul? How would you describe this part of you? If you do not believe this to be the case, how do you explain the source of your individual personality?

Have you ever heard the voice of God? What were the circumstances? Is there a particular time, place, or state of mind that is most conducive to being open to God?

Close Study of the Original Text

This is a long story, so focus on Genesis 28:10–22: Jacob's ladder. After the story has been read, invite discussion of the following questions.

This was Jacob's first vision of God. What do you think made Jacob able to perceive God at this time?

Jacob had a quid pro quo relationship with God. In other words, if God kept Jacob safe, then Jacob was willing to let this deity be his God. What is your impression about this view of God? Is it common?

What do you think the ladder represents?

Reading "The Trickster Transformed"

If the class has not already read the story, teacher should either read it out loud, put students in small groups to read it to each other, or allow fifteen minutes for students to read it silently. After the story has been read, invite discussion of the following questions.

Rebecca believed that a leader must be a visionary. What are the pluses and minuses of leadership by such a person?

Jacob discovered God when he was in the wilderness at the low point of his life. Why do you think he was open to God at that time and place?

Jacob fooled his brother and father and then he himself was fooled by Laban. Do you think this biblical notion of what goes around comes around is accurate? Can you think of any examples of this from your life?

Both Jacob and Esau matured in this story. What caused each one of them to grow up?

Creative Activities

Do one of the following activities.

Recast an incident from the conflict between Jacob and Esau to star two sisters rather than two brothers. Retell the incident featuring these female characters.

Dramatize the story with a technique known as Freeze Tag. Have students act out a scene of the story. During the reenactment, a student who is watching the scene yells, "Freeze." The actors freeze in their positions. The student who yelled taps one of the actors on the shoulder and takes his or her place. The scene begins again with the new actor saying or doing something that redirects how it was being played.

Closure

After reading "The Trickster Transformed" and a biblical story about Jacob, do you feel differently about this patriarch?

Joseph's
School

Themes

Going down in order to come up

The process of maturation

Dreams

Opener

Do the following journaling exercise.

Describe a time in your life when something good came out of something bad.

Close Study of the Original Text

Focus on the beginning of the text. Read Genesis 37:1–17. (The word *na-ar* is often translated from Hebrew as "helper." In this case, however, it actually refers to a boy younger than thirteen.) Ask students to make a psychological profile of Joseph based on these verses. Questions to consider:

Why is a seventeen-year-old described as a *na-ar?*

What did Jacob do to encourage the hatred that Joseph's brothers felt toward Joseph?

What was odd about the man Joseph found in the fields?

Reading "Joseph's School"

If the class has not already read the story, teacher should either read it out loud, put students in small groups to read it to each other, or allow fifteen minutes for students to read it silently. After the story has been read, invite discussion of the following questions.

Joseph had to go down into an Egyptian prison in order to free his spirit and change who he was. Rabbi Nachman of Breslov, an important Jewish thinker of the early nineteenth-century, taught that one must "go down in order to come up." Do you think this idea is often true today, just as it is in Joseph's story?

Dreams were once believed to be prophetic, but in the modern age they have lost much of their significance. Do you think dreams can carry messages, even today?

The angel Gabriella helped Joseph locate his brothers. In Hebrew, the words *angel* and *messenger* are the same. Has an "angel," either human or divine, ever helped you?

"Joseph's School" contends that both Joseph and the Hebrew nation needed to go down to Egypt for essentially the same reason. Do you agree? Why or why not?

Creative Activities

Do one of the following activities.

Working in groups, students should take a large piece of butcher paper and draw the outline of a body. They should paint or color Joseph's coat on this form. Elements of Joseph's personality should be represented in its decoration, either through words or symbols.

Choose a character other than Joseph and write a scene from the Joseph story in that character's point of view.

Closure

Every student demonstrates with a facial expression or body posture how Joseph might have felt when he was thrown into the pit.

God's Stutterer

Themes

Disabilities as strengths

Leadership

Selflessness

Opener

Do one of the following activities.

Divide the class into groups of five. Give each group a sheet of butcher paper. Instruct each group to list three effective political leaders and a few traits that make these leaders successful. Bring the class back together and share the leaders and their traits. See if there are any common ideas or traits.

In their journals, students should describe a person they know who has a disability and explain how this person has used his or her disability to his or her advantage. If students don't know of a real person to whom this applies, they should write about a character from literature or film.

Close Study of the Original Text

There are four chapters of biblical text that should be read in conjunction with this story—Exodus 1–4:16. As it will take too long for every student to read the entire story, a good technique to use here is jigsaw-reading. Break the class into four groups. Each group reads a single chapter and summarizes the chapter in two or three sentences. After five minutes, the class reconvenes and groups share their summaries. After jigsaw-reading the story, invite discussion of the following questions.

Why do you think God chose a leader with a speech disability?

The midwives risked their lives to save Hebrew babies, and then they lied to Pharaoh about their actions. Are there any situations in which you would be willing to risk your life?

How did growing up in Pharaoh's court help Moses become a leader?

How was Moses's character shaped when he killed the Egyptian, when he ran away from the two fighting Hebrews, and when he defended the shepherd girls?

Reading "God's Stutterer"

Teacher should *not* assign this story to be read the week before. Rather, teacher should blindfold the students and read the story to them so they can experience a disability. After the story has been read, invite discussion of the following questions.

How was listening to a story blindfolded different from listening to a story with your eyes open?

When God approached Moses, Moses didn't want to leave his nice life as a shepherd to lead a rebellion. Have you ever felt called upon to do something that required you to sacrifice some part of your life?

According to "God's Stutterer," the lesson of the Burning Bush is that Moses was able to look beneath the surface reality of the bush to see the Divine Spark because he felt so at peace with the world. Do you think the Burning Bush might have had some other lesson to teach? If so, what?

The three most prominent qualities of Moses's character in this story were compassion, backbone, and humility. Do you think these are important qualities for leaders to have? What other traits do you think a leader should possess?

Gabriella and God had very different views of the human species. Summarize both of their views. Do you agree with one of them? Why or why not?

In "God's Stutterer," God didn't want to do all the work of rescuing the Hebrews. Instead, God called upon Moses to lead the Hebrews out of slavery, giving the Hebrew people a sense of accomplishment and of taking active roles in their own fates. However, in the Passover Haggadah, which is a midrash on the same biblical story, Moses is not mentioned once. According to the Haggadah, God alone rescued the Hebrews. Why do you think these two midrashim deal so differently with the role of God? Is there any other way to think about the role God played in the Exodus?

Creative Activities

Do one of the following activities.

Divide the class into groups of four. Assign each group a different disability, such as blindness, deafness, and so on. Each group should then write and perform a dramatization of a section of the story, replacing Moses's stutter with a different disability.

Divide the class into groups of four. Assign each group to rewrite a different biblical scene giving a main character a disability. Have students perform the dramatization.

Closure

Now that you have learned about Moses and his stutter, do you see disabilities in a new light? If so, how has your perception of them changed?

The
Argument

Themes

Justice versus mercy

Repentance

Fleeing from God

Opener

Do one of the following journaling exercises.

God is called by a number of names in the Hebrew Bible. The two most often used names are Elohim and the unpronounceable YHVH. In Jewish tradition, Elohim represents God's justice, while YHVH represents God's mercy. Which aspect of God do you think is more important in the current world? Why?

Most Hebrew prophets were ignored by the people of Israel. Why were they ignored? In today's world are there "prophets" that speak about important issues, but are ignored?

Close Study of the Original Text

Read chapters 1 and 3–4 of Jonah. (If students are familiar with this story, only read 1:1–6 and 4:1–11.) After the story has been read, invite discussion of the following questions.

Why did Jonah flee from God?

What, if anything, happens today to a person that tries to flee from his or her responsibility?

What do you think God was trying to prove to Jonah in chapter 4?

While most Hebrew prophets were ignored, the Ninevites repented and changed their ways after Jonah said, "In forty days Nineveh will be overturned." Why might the Ninevites have quickly done what the Hebrews rarely did?

In the Hebrew Bible, Jonah's movements in chapter 1:1–6, are all going downward. Jonah goes down to Jaffa, down into the ship, and down into the hold. What might this signify?

Reading "The Argument"

If the class has not already read the story, teacher should either read it out loud, put students in small groups to read it to each other, or allow fifteen minutes for students to read it silently. After the story has been read, invite discussion of the following questions.

Do you think any parts of "The Argument" were true to the original story? If yes, did any part of "The Argument" clarify the original story for you?

God spared Nineveh and then the descendants of the Ninevites went on to destroy ten of Israel's twelve tribes. Was Jonah right after all about the fate that the Ninevites deserved?

God tried to teach Jonah that mercy trumps justice, but Jonah believed it should be the other way around. What do you think?

Have a few words ever changed your life?

Creative Activities

Do one of the following activities.

Up in heaven, God and Jonah have just witnessed the destruction of the ten tribes. Write their dialogue.

Take a large piece of butcher paper and divide it in half. On the first half, draw pictures of Ninevites before they repented. On the second half, draw pictures of them after they repented.

Write a play in which God approaches a modern-day Jonah, asking him to prophesy the downfall of the United States or another country or people.

Closure

Just as Jonah proclaimed one sentence to the Ninevites, have each student proclaim one sentence about the story of Jonah.

Source

Tanhuma Wa-Yikra 8

Uncorked Perfume

Themes

Assimilation

Intermarriage

Beauty as power

God operating behind the scenes

Opener

Do one of the following journaling exercises.

Have you ever experienced a coincidence that is difficult to explain rationally? How might you explain it?

Queen Esther's gift was her beauty. What gift(s) do you possess?

Close Study of the Original Text

The story is too long to read, so jigsaw the reading of chapters 1–8. Have students look for instances where God may be directing the action from behind the scenes. Inform students that while the original Hebrew text doesn't mention God's presence, the first translation of the Bible, the Septuagint, inserts God into the story numerous times. After jigsaw-reading this story, invite discussion of the following questions.

Was God operating behind the scenes in this story?

Do you think God operates behind the scenes in real life?

How was intermarriage dealt with in the book of Esther? In modern times, is intermarriage an issue? What are the pros and cons of marrying outside one's religious or ethnic group?

Haman was portrayed as all evil in the story but people aren't wholly good or wholly evil. If you were to write a story about Haman, what examples of his personality or how he lived his life could you include to create a more balanced character?

Reading "Uncorked Perfume"

If the class has not already read the story, teacher should either read it out loud, put students in small groups to read it to each other, or allow fifteen minutes for students to read it silently. After the story has been read, invite discussion of the following questions.

Is beauty a source of power for women? For men?

Esther implied to Mordechai that beauty is more important and more powerful than Torah study. Do you agree? Why or why not?

Esther claimed that men are more concerned with a woman's beauty than with what is inside her heart or head. Is there any truth to this claim?

Gabriella commented that humans pretend to do good in order to cover the tracks of their evil. Give a real-life example of this.

Tell how a real-life person used his or her "gift from God" to help others.

As soon as she became queen, Esther stopped following Jewish law. If you were no longer living in your family or community, do you think you would change your way of life?

Creative Activities

Do one of the following activities.

Dramatize the following scenario: After Queen Esther's story became public, many Persian Jews started intermarrying. Mordechai became fearful that the Jews would assimilate completely into Persian culture and asked Queen Esther to do something about it.

Rather than beauty, assign Esther a different trait, such as intelligence or physical strength, and have her use this new trait to rescue the Jews.

Closure

Go around the room and have students fill in the blanks: "Esther was a _____," "Haman was a _____," and "Mordechai was a _____."

The Last
Lesson

Themes

Theodicy (defense of God's goodness in light of the existence of evil)

Tikkun Olam (Hebrew for "repairing the world." A basic precept of Judaism is the world is flawed and it is up to humans to return the world to its pristine state.)

Opener

Do one of the following journaling exercises.

Are good people usually rewarded for being good? Do bad things happen to good people? Use examples from real life to explain your answers.

Describe a time when you or someone you knew was a victim of divine injustice. How did you feel about it? Did this affect your relationship with God?

Close Study of the Original Text

Divide into four groups and jigsaw-read the book of Ruth. After the story has been read, invite discussion of the following questions.

Why might have God caused Naomi to suffer so much misfortune in chapter 1?

Why did Ruth accompany Naomi back to Bethlehem instead of staying in Moab?

What does this story suggest about the stereotype that women are always passive in male-female relationships?

The story has a happy ending with the birth of Obed. Does this ending reflect what happens in the real world?

Few biblical stories have happy endings. Why do you think this is?

Reading "The Last Lesson"

If the class has not already read the story, teacher should either read it out loud, put students in small groups to read it to each other, or allow fifteen minutes for students to read it silently. After the story has been read, invite discussion of the following questions.

Naomi argued that punishment from God is arbitrary. The Bethlemite women insisted that punishment comes in payment for something. What was Naomi's view at the end of the story? Do you agree with any of these ideas about why bad things happen?

Naomi's friend said that Naomi was punished because her sons married Moabites. Why didn't Naomi believe her?

Both Ruth and Naomi found only silence when they sought comfort or advice from heaven. Have you ever been in a difficult situation and sought God? What happened?

Did Naomi ever make peace with God?

Creative Activities

Do one of the following activities.

Choose a historical event (such as the Holocaust) or another type of tragedy (such as a child dying of cancer) and have the class stage a mock trial of God to decide if God is culpable. Assign the roles of judge, prosecuting attorney, defense attorney, jury, witnesses for both the defense and prosecution, and God.

Make a two-sided mural on a large piece of butcher paper. One side should depict problems in the world. The other side should depict ways that students can change the world by working toward solutions to these problems.

Closure

The last lesson was that we don't need to accept the world as it is because it can be changed. What about the world is not acceptable to you? How can you change it?

The Suicide Bomber

Themes

Religious fanaticism

Morality in leadership

Self-confidence

Political leadership as military might

Opener

Do one of the following journaling activities.

Should a political leader be held to a higher level of morality than the average citizen? Why or why not?

What are some reasons a person might give for becoming a suicide bomber?

Close Study of the Original Text

Divide into four groups and jigsaw-read Judges 13–16. After the story has been read, invite discussion of the following questions.

What do you think the nation of Israel did that made God abandon it at the beginning of this story?

Do you think that becoming a Nazirite or taking up any other religious vow brings a person closer to God?

Many Jewish scholars believe that Samson's suicide was a positive action. Do you agree?

Biblical stories often involve a woman who is having difficulty getting pregnant. Why do you think this situation is a biblical motif?

What is the purpose of the scene featuring the bees, honey, and the lion about?

Describe Samson's key character traits. Would they make him a good political leader today?

The Bible explains that Samson lost his power when God departed from him after his hair was cut. Can you think of an alternative reason why having his hair cut made Samson weak?

Reading "The Suicide Bomber"

This is a longer story and may be difficult to read in a class period of less than one hour. Teacher can either jigsaw the reading of it or assign it as homework prior to the class in which it will be discussed. After the story has been read, invite discussion of the following questions.

Compare Samson's suicide to those of modern suicide bombers.

Israel overlooked Samson's philandering because he kept Israel safe. Should a leader's personal morality be considered independently of his or her work?

The story argues that Samson's real power was not in his hair, but rather in the confidence he lost when his hair was cut. Do you think this could be true?

Samson always paid the Philistine back more than he got. Is this a good military tactic? Why or why not?

God bemoaned that there is nothing sadder than being used as an inspiration for carnage. Is it possible to dissuade people from using God as their motivation for destruction? If so, how?

Creative Activities

Do one of the following activities.

Have students write and perform a modern-day version of a scene from Samson's story.

Have students rewrite the story from the point of view of Delilah or another Philistine.

Closure

Did "The Suicide Bomber" make you rethink how you view biblical heroes?

The Second Sling

Themes

Sexuality

Leadership and moral impairment

Reconciliation of differing biblical stories

Opener

Draw the outline of King David on butcher paper and hang it on the wall. Give students markers and direct them to write something that they know about King David on the figure. Read their responses.

Close Study of the Original Text

David occupies more verses in the Hebrew Bible than any other biblical character, so a complete reading of his story is not possible. Read only the beginning of the David story and the second account of Goliath's death, found in 1 Samuel 16–17:53 and 2 Samuel 21:18–19. After the story has been read, invite discussion of the following questions.

Which of David's characteristics made him God's choice to be king?

Can you explain why Goliath was killed twice?

What do you think David was feeling as he faced Goliath?

While many people expressed their love for David, David only expressed his love for one person—Jonathan. What do you think this means?

Reading "The Second Sling"

This is a longer story and may be difficult to read in a class period of less than one hour. Teacher can either jigsaw the reading of it or assign the story as homework prior to the class in which it will be discussed. After the story has been read, invite discussion of the following questions.

Do you think the explanation in "The Second Sling" adequately solves the problem of Goliath being killed twice?

"The Second Sling" implies that David was bisexual. Do you think the biblical version of this story supports this view?

If David was bisexual, why might the Bible cover up this fact?

Was God's punishment sufficient for David's adultery and the murder he committed?

Can you think of any great historical figures whose moral failures are known?

Creative Aspect

Do one of the following activities.

Students write their own psalm to God using the poetic or musical technique of their choice.

Write a midrash about an incident of David's life, focusing on his personality.

Stage the scene of Goliath's death.

Closure

While David was a flawed man, both God and Gabriella recognized his greatness. What do you think?

Wrap-up Activities

Review the Stories

Have students fill out the handout on pp. 35–36. Discuss their answers as a class.

Writing Midrash

Have students write a complete midrash on a biblical story not included in *The Triumph of Eve*.

The Triumph of Eve—Review

For each story, list the major themes and messages. Do you think each title fits the story it belongs to? Why or why not? What did you think of each story?

"The Triumph of Eve"

"Cain's Co-Defendant"

"Noah's Cracked Rainbow"

"Reasonable Faith"

"The Trickster Transformed"

"Joseph's School"

"God's Stutterer"

"The Argument"

"Uncorked Perfume"

"The Last Lesson"

"The Suicide Bomber"

"The Second Sling"

Children's Spirituality—Board Books

How Did the Animals Help God? (A Board Book)
by Nancy Sohn Swartz, Full-color illus. by Melanie Hall
Abridged from Nancy Sohn Swartz's *In Our Image,* God asks all of nature to offer gifts to humankind—with a promise that they will care for creation in return.
5 x 5, 24 pp, Board Book, Full-color illus., ISBN 1-59473-044-X **$7.99** *For ages 0–4*

Where Is God? (A Board Book)
by Lawrence and Karen Kushner; Full-color illus. by Dawn W. Majewski
A gentle way for young children to explore how God is with us every day, in every way. Abridged from *Because Nothing Looks Like God* by Lawrence and Karen Kushner.   5 x 5, 24 pp, Board, Full-color illus., ISBN 1-893361-17-9 **$7.99** *For ages 0–4*

What Does God Look Like? (A Board Book)
by Lawrence and Karen Kushner; Full-color illus. by Dawn W. Majewski
A simple way for young children to explore the ways that we "see" God. Abridged from *Because Nothing Looks Like God* by Lawrence and Karen Kushner.
5 x 5, 24 pp, Board, Full-color illus., ISBN 1-893361-23-3 **$7.95** *For ages 0–4*

How Does God Make Things Happen? (A Board Book)
by Lawrence and Karen Kushner; Full-color illus. by Dawn W. Majewski
A charming invitation for young children to explore how God makes things happen in our world. Abridged from *Because Nothing Looks Like God* by Lawrence and Karen Kushner.   5 x 5, 24 pp, Board, Full-color illus., ISBN 1-893361-24-1 **$7.95** *For ages 0–4*

What Is God's Name? (A Board Book)
by Sandy Eisenberg Sasso; Full-color illus. by Phoebe Stone
Everyone and everything in the world has a name. What is God's name? Abridged from the award-winning *In God's Name* by Sandy Eisenberg Sasso.
5 x 5, 24 pp, Board, Full-color illus., ISBN 1-893361-10-1 **$7.99** *For ages 0–4*

What You Will See Inside ...

This important new series of books is designed to show children ages 6–10 the Who, What, When, Where, Why and How of traditional houses of worship, liturgical celebrations, and rituals of different world faiths, empowering them to respect and understand their own religious traditions—and those of their friends and neighbors.

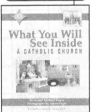

What You Will See Inside a Catholic Church
by Reverend Michael Keane; Foreword by Robert J. Keeley, Ed.D.
Full-color photographs by Aaron Pepis
A colorful, fun-to-read introduction to the traditions of Catholic worship and faith. Visually explains the common use of the altar, processional cross, baptismal font, votive candles, and more.   8½ x 10½, 32 pp, HC, ISBN 1-893361-54-3 **$17.95**
Also available in Spanish: **Lo que se puede ver dentro de una iglesia católica**
   8½ x 10½, 32 pp, Full-color photos, HC, ISBN 1-893361-66-7 **$16.95**

What You Will See Inside a Mosque
by Aisha Karen Khan; Photographs by Aaron Pepis
Featuring full-page pictures and concise descriptions of what is happening, the objects used, the spiritual leaders and laypeople who have specific roles, and the spiritual intent of the believers. Demystifies the celebrations and ceremonies of Islam throughout the year.
8½ x 10½, 32 pp, Full-color photos, HC, ISBN 1-893361-60-8 **$16.95**

What You Will See Inside a Synagogue
by Rabbi Lawrence A. Hoffman and Dr. Ron Wolfson; Full-color photos by Bill Aron
A colorful, fun-to-read introduction that explains the ways and whys of Jewish worship and religious life. Full-page photos; concise but informative descriptions of the objects used, the clergy and laypeople who have specific roles, and much more.
8½ x 10½, 32 pp, Full-color photos, HC, ISBN 1-59473-012-1 **$17.99**

Children's Spirituality

ENDORSED BY CATHOLIC, PROTESTANT, JEWISH, AND BUDDHIST RELIGIOUS LEADERS

God Said Amen
by Sandy Eisenberg Sasso; Full-color illus. by Avi Katz
A warm and inspiring tale of two kingdoms that shows us that we need only reach out to each other to find the answers to our prayers.
9 x 12, 32 pp, HC, Full-color illus., ISBN 1-58023-080-6 **$16.95**
For ages 4 & up (a Jewish Lights book)

How Does God Listen?
by Kay Lindahl; Full-color photo illus. by Cynthia Maloney
How do we know when God is listening to us? Children will find the answers to these questions as they engage their senses while the story unfolds, learning how God listens in the wind, waves, clouds, hot chocolate, perfume, our tears and our laughter.
10 x 8½, 32 pp, Quality PB, Full-color photo illus., ISBN 1-59473-084-9 **$8.99**
For ages 3–6

In God's Name
by Sandy Eisenberg Sasso; Full-color illus. by Phoebe Stone
Like an ancient myth in its poetic text and vibrant illustrations, this award-winning modern fable about the search for God's name celebrates the diversity and, at the same time, the unity of all the people of the world.
9 x 12, 32 pp, HC, Full-color illus., ISBN 1-879045-26-5 **$16.95**
For ages 4 & up (a Jewish Lights book)

Also available in Spanish:
El nombre de Dios
9 x 12, 32 pp, HC, Full-color illus., ISBN 1-893361-63-2 **$16.95**

Where Does God Live?
by August Gold; Full-color photo illus. by Matthew J. Perlman
Using simple, everyday examples that children can relate to, this colorful book helps young readers develop a personal understanding of God.
10 x 8½, 32 pp, Quality PB, Full-color photo illus., ISBN 1-893361-39-X **$8.99**
For ages 3–6

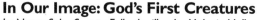

In Our Image: God's First Creatures
by Nancy Sohn Swartz; Full-color illus. by Melanie Hall
A playful new twist on the Creation story—from the perspective of the animals. Celebrates the interconnectedness of nature and the harmony of all living things.   9 x 12, 32 pp, HC, Full-color illus., ISBN 1-879045-99-0 **$16.95**
For ages 4 & up (a Jewish Lights book)

Noah's Wife: The Story of Naamah
by Sandy Eisenberg Sasso; Full-color illus. by Bethanne Andersen
This new story, based on an ancient text, opens readers' religious imaginations to new ideas about the well-known story of the Flood. When God tells Noah to bring the animals of the world onto the ark, God also calls on Naamah, Noah's wife, to save each plant on Earth.
9 x 12, 32 pp, HC, Full-color illus., ISBN 1-58023-134-9 **$16.95**
For ages 4 & up (a Jewish Lights book)

Also available:
Naamah: Noah's Wife (A Board Book)
by Sandy Eisenberg Sasso, Full-color illus by Bethanne Andersen
5 x 5, 24 pp, Board Book, Full-color illus., ISBN 1-893361-56-X **$7.99** *For ages 0–4*

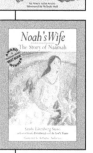

Children's Spirituality

Because Nothing Looks Like God

by Lawrence and Karen Kushner; Full-color illus. by Dawn W. Majewski

Real-life examples of happiness and sadness—from goodnight stories, to the hope and fear felt the first time at bat, to the closing moments of life—introduce children to the possibilities of spiritual life.

11 x 8½, 32 pp, HC, Full-color illus., ISBN 1-58023-092-X **$16.95**

For ages 4 & up (a Jewish Lights book)

Also available:

Teacher's Guide, 8½ x 11, 22 pp, PB, ISBN 1-58023-140-3 **$6.95** *For ages 5–8*

Becoming Me: A Story of Creation

by Martin Boroson; Full-color illus. by Christopher Gilvan-Cartwright

Told in the personal "voice" of the Creator, here is a story about creation and relationship that is about each one of us.

8 x 10, 32 pp, Full-color illus., HC, ISBN 1-893361-11-X **$16.95** *For ages 4 & up*

But God Remembered: Stories of Women from Creation to the Promised Land   *by Sandy Eisenberg Sasso; Full-color illus. by Bethanne Andersen*

A fascinating collection of four different stories of women only briefly mentioned in biblical tradition and religious texts; all teach important values through their actions and faith.   9 x 12, 32 pp, HC, Full-color illus., ISBN 1-879045-43-5 **$16.95**

For ages 8 & up (a Jewish Lights book)

Cain & Abel: Finding the Fruits of Peace

by Sandy Eisenberg Sasso; Full-color illus. by Joani Keller Rothenberg

A sensitive recasting of the ancient tale shows we have the power to deal with anger in positive ways. Provides questions for kids and adults to explore together. "Editor's Choice"—American Library Association's *Booklist*

9 x 12, 32 pp, HC, Full-color illus., ISBN 1-58023-123-3 **$16.95** *For ages 5 & up (a Jewish Lights book)*

Does God Hear My Prayer?

by August Gold; Full-color photo illus. by Diane Hardy Waller

This colorful book introduces preschoolers as well as young readers to prayer and how prayer can help them express their own fears, wants, sadness, surprise, and joy.   10 x 8½, 32 pp, Quality PB, Full-color photo illus., ISBN 1-59473-102-0 **$8.99**

The 11th Commandment: Wisdom from Our Children

by The Children of America

"If there were an Eleventh Commandment, what would it be?" Children of many religious denominations across America answer this question—in their own drawings and words. "A rare book of spiritual celebration for all people, of all ages, for all time." —*Bookviews*

8 x 10, 48 pp, HC, Full-color illus., ISBN 1-879045-46-X **$16.95** *For ages 4 & up (a Jewish Lights book)*

For Heaven's Sake

by Sandy Eisenberg Sasso; Full-color illus. by Kathryn Kunz Finney

Everyone talked about heaven: "Thank heavens." "Heaven forbid." "For heaven's sake, Isaiah." But no one would say what heaven was or how to find it. So Isaiah decides to find out, by seeking answers from many different people.

9 x 12, 32 pp, HC, Full-color illus., ISBN 1-58023-054-7 **$16.95** *For ages 4 & up (a Jewish Lights book)*

God in Between

by Sandy Eisenberg Sasso; Full-color illus. by Sally Sweetland

If you wanted to find God, where would you look? A magical, mythical tale that teaches that God can be found where we are: within all of us and the relationships between us.   9 x 12, 32 pp, HC, Full-color illus., ISBN 1-879045-86-9 **$16.95**

For ages 4 & up (a Jewish Lights book)

Children's Spiritual Biography

Ten Amazing People
And How They Changed the World
by Maura D. Shaw; Foreword by Dr. Robert Coles
Full-color illus. by Stephen Marchesi

For ages 7 & up

Black Elk • Dorothy Day • Malcolm X • Mahatma Gandhi • Martin Luther King, Jr. • Mother Teresa • Janusz Korczak • Desmond Tutu • Thich Nhat Hanh • Albert Schweitzer

This vivid, inspirational, and authoritative book will open new possibilities for children by telling the stories of how ten of the past century's greatest leaders changed the world in important ways.

8½ x 11, 48 pp, HC, Full-color illus., ISBN 1-893361-47-0 **$17.95** *For ages 7 & up*

Spiritual Biographies for Young People—For ages 7 and up

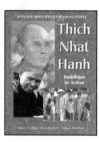 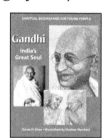  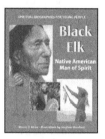

Black Elk: Native American Man of Spirit
by Maura D. Shaw; Full-color illus. by Stephen Marchesi
Through historically accurate illustrations and photos, inspiring age-appropriate activities, and Black Elk's own words, this colorful biography introduces children to a remarkable person who ensured that the traditions and beliefs of his people would not be forgotten.
6¾ x 8¾, 32 pp, HC, Full-color illus., ISBN 1-59473-043-1 **$12.99**

Dorothy Day: A Catholic Life of Action
by Maura D. Shaw; Full-color illus. by Stephen Marchesi
Introduces children to one of the most inspiring women of the twentieth century, a down-to-earth spiritual leader who saw the presence of God in every person she met. Includes practical activities, a timeline, and a list of important words to know.
6¾ x 8¾, 32 pp, HC, Full-color illus., ISBN 1-59473-011-3 **$12.99**

Gandhi: India's Great Soul
by Maura D. Shaw; Full-color illus. by Stephen Marchesi
There are a number of biographies of Gandhi written for young readers, but this is the only one that balances a simple text with illustrations, photographs, and activities that encourage children and adults to talk about how to make changes happen without violence. Introduces children to important concepts of freedom, equality, and justice among people of all backgrounds and religions.
6¾ x 8¾, 32 pp, HC, Full-color illus., ISBN 1-893361-91-8 **$12.95**

Thich Nhat Hanh: Buddhism in Action
by Maura D. Shaw; Full-color illus. by Stephen Marchesi
Warm illustrations, photos, age-appropriate activities, and Thich Nhat Hanh's own poems introduce a great man to children in a way they can understand and enjoy. Includes a list of important Buddhist words to know.
6¾ x 8¾, 32 pp, HC, Full-color illus., ISBN 1-893361-87-X **$12.95**

Spiritual Practice

Divining the Body
Reclaim the Holiness of Your Physical Self *by Jan Phillips*
A practical and inspiring guidebook for connecting the body and soul in spiritual practice. Leads you into a milieu of reverence, mystery, and delight, helping you discover a redeemed sense of self.
8 x 8, 256 pp, Quality PB, ISBN 1-59473-080-6 **$16.99**

Finding Time for the Timeless
Spirituality in the Workweek *by John McQuiston II*
Simple, refreshing stories that provide you with examples of how you can refocus and enrich your daily life using prayer or meditation, ritual, and other forms of spiritual practice. 5½ x 6½, 208 pp, HC, ISBN 1-59473-035-0 **$17.99**

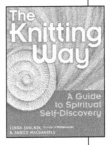

The Gospel of Thomas: A Guidebook for Spiritual Practice
by Ron Miller; Translations by Stevan Davies
An innovative guide to bring a new spiritual classic into daily life. Offers a way to translate the wisdom of the Gospel of Thomas into daily practice, manifesting in your life the same consciousness revealed in Jesus of Nazareth. Written for readers of all religious backgrounds, this guidebook will help you to apply Jesus's wisdom to your own life and to the world around you.
6 x 9, 160 pp, Quality PB, ISBN 1-59473-047-4 **$14.99**

The Knitting Way: A Guide to Spiritual Self-Discovery
by Linda Skolnik and Janice MacDaniels
Through sharing stories, hands-on explorations, and daily cultivation, Skolnik and MacDaniels help you see beyond the surface of a simple craft in order to discover ways in which nuances of knitting can apply to the larger scheme of life and spirituality. Includes original knitting patterns.
7 x 9, 240 pp, Quality PB, ISBN 1-59473-079-2 **$16.99**

Earth, Water, Fire, and Air: Essential Ways of Connecting to Spirit
by Cait Johnson   6 x 9, 224 pp, HC, ISBN 1-893361-65-9 **$19.95**

Forty Days to Begin a Spiritual Life
Today's Most Inspiring Teachers Help You on Your Way
Edited by Maura Shaw and the Editors at SkyLight Paths; Foreword by Dan Wakefield
7 x 9, 144 pp, Quality PB, ISBN 1-893361-48-9 **$16.95**

Labyrinths from the Outside In
Walking to Spiritual Insight—A Beginner's Guide
by Donna Schaper and Carole Ann Camp
6 x 9, 208 pp, b/w illus. and photographs, Quality PB, ISBN 1-893361-18-7 **$16.95**

Practicing the Sacred Art of Listening: A Guide to Enrich Your Relationships
and Kindle Your Spiritual Life—The Listening Center Workshop
by Kay Lindahl   8 x 8, 176 pp, Quality PB, ISBN 1-893361-85-3 **$16.95**

The Sacred Art of Bowing: Preparing to Practice
by Andi Young   5½ x 8½, 128 pp, b/w illus., Quality PB, ISBN 1-893361-82-9 **$14.95**

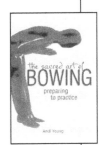

The Sacred Art of Chant: Preparing to Practice
by Ana Hernandez   5½ x 8½, 192 pp, Quality PB, ISBN 1-59473-036-9 **$15.99**

The Sacred Art of Fasting: Preparing to Practice
by Thomas Ryan, CSP   5½ x 8½, 192 pp, Quality PB, ISBN 1-59473-078-4 **$15.99**

The Sacred Art of Listening: Forty Reflections for Cultivating a Spiritual Practice
by Kay Lindahl; Illustrations by Amy Schnapper
8 x 8, 160 pp, Illus., Quality PB, ISBN 1-893361-44-6 **$16.99**

Sacred Speech: A Practical Guide for Keeping Spirit in Your Speech
by Rev. Donna Schaper   6 x 9, 176 pp, Quality PB, ISBN 1-59473-068-7 **$15.99**;
HC, ISBN 1-893361-74-8 **$21.95**

Midrash Fiction

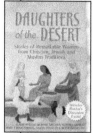

Daughters of the Desert: Tales of Remarkable Women from Christian, Jewish, and Muslim Traditions   *by Claire Rudolf Murphy, Meghan Nuttall Sayres, Mary Cronk Farrell, Sarah Conover, and Betsy Wharton*

Breathes new life into the old tales of our female ancestors in faith. Uses traditional scriptural passages as starting points, then with vivid detail fills in historical context and place. Chapters reveal the voices of Sarah, Hagar, Huldah, Esther, Salome, Mary Magdalene, Lydia, Khadija, Fatima, and many more. Historical fiction ideal for readers of all ages. Quality paperback includes reader's discussion guide.

5½ x 8½, 208 pp, Quality PB, ISBN 1-59473-106-3 **$14.99**; HC, 192 pp, ISBN 1-893361-72-1 **$19.95**

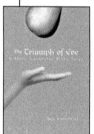

The Triumph of Eve & Other Subversive Bible Tales
by Matt Biers-Ariel

Many people were taught and remember only a one-dimensional Bible. These engaging retellings are the antidote to this—they're witty, often hilarious, always profound, and invite you to grapple with questions and issues that are often hidden in the original text.

5½ x 8½, 192 pp, HC, ISBN 1-59473-040-7 **$19.99**

Religious Etiquette / Reference

How to Be a Perfect Stranger, 3rd Edition: The Essential Religious Etiquette Handbook   *Edited by Stuart M. Matlins and Arthur J. Magida*

The indispensable guidebook to help the well-meaning guest when visiting other people's religious ceremonies. A straightforward guide to the rituals and celebrations of the major religions and denominations in the United States and Canada from the perspective of an interested guest of any other faith, based on information obtained from authorities of each religion. Belongs in every living room, library, and office. Covers:

African American Methodist Churches • Assemblies of God • Baha'i • Baptist • Buddhist • Christian Church (Disciples of Christ) • Christian Science (Church of Christ, Scientist) • Churches of Christ • Episcopalian and Anglican • Hindu • Islam • Jehovah's Witnesses • Jewish • Lutheran • Mennonite/Amish • Methodist • Mormon (Church of Jesus Christ of Latter-day Saints) • Native American/First Nations • Orthodox Churches • Pentecostal Church of God • Presbyterian • Quaker (Religious Society of Friends) • Reformed Church in America/Canada • Roman Catholic • Seventh-day Adventist • Sikh • Unitarian Universalist • United Church of Canada • United Church of Christ

6 x 9, 432 pp, Quality PB, ISBN 1-893361-67-5 **$19.95**

The Perfect Stranger's Guide to Funerals and Grieving Practices: A Guide to Etiquette in Other People's Religious Ceremonies   *Edited by Stuart M. Matlins*
6 x 9, 240 pp, Quality PB, ISBN 1-893361-20-9 **$16.95**

The Perfect Stranger's Guide to Wedding Ceremonies: A Guide to Etiquette in Other People's Religious Ceremonies   *Edited by Stuart M. Matlins*
6 x 9, 208 pp, Quality PB, ISBN 1-893361-19-5 **$16.95**

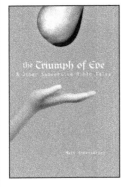
Order Form

Check enclosed for $_____ payable to

SkyLight Paths Publishing

or

Charge my credit card: ❏ VISA ❏ MASTERCARD

Card # _____

Exp. date_____ CID#_____

Signature _____

Name _____ Phone_____

Street _____

City / State / Zip_____

Discount Schedule for Quantity Orders	
Copies of the <u>SAME</u> book	Discount
3–6	10%
7–14	20%
15–24	25%
25–49	30%
50+	35%

#Book	Title	ISBN	Price	Total
____	_____	_____	$ _____	$ _____
____	_____	_____	$ _____	$ _____
____	_____	_____	$ _____	$ _____
____	_____	_____	$ _____	$ _____

Minus Discount_____ % <$_____>

Subtotal $_____

Shipping and handling (Add $3.95 for the first book, $2.00 ea. add'l book to a maximum of $20.00) $_____

TOTAL $_____

Or phone, fax, mail or e-mail to: **SKYLIGHT PATHS Publishing**
Sunset Farm Offices, Route 4 • P.O. Box 237 • Woodstock, Vermont 05091
Tel: (802) 457-4000 • Fax: (802) 457-4004 • www.skylightpaths.com
Credit card orders: (800) 962-4544 (8:30AM–5:30PM ET Monday–Friday)
Generous discounts on quantity orders. SATISFACTION GUARANTEED. Prices subject to change.

About SKYLIGHT PATHS Publishing

SkyLight Paths Publishing is creating a place where people of different spiritual traditions come together for challenge and inspiration, a place where we can help each other understand the mystery that lies at the heart of our existence.

Through spirituality, our religious beliefs are increasingly becoming a part of our lives—rather than *apart* from our lives. While many of us may be more interested than ever in spiritual growth, we may be less firmly planted in traditional religion. Yet, we do want to deepen our relationship to the sacred, to learn from our own as well as from other faith traditions, and to practice in new ways.

SkyLight Paths sees both believers and seekers as a community that increasingly transcends traditional boundaries of religion and denomination—people wanting to learn from each other, *walking together, finding the way.*

For your information and convenience, at the back of this book we have provided a list of other SkyLight Paths books you might find interesting and useful. They cover the following subjects:

Buddhism / Zen	Gnosticism	Mysticism
Catholicism	Hinduism /	Poetry
Children's Books	Vedanta	Prayer
Christianity	Inspiration	Religious Etiquette
Comparative	Islam / Sufism	Retirement
Religion	Judaism / Kabbalah /	Spiritual Biography
Current Events	Enneagram	Spiritual Direction
Earth-Based	Meditation	Spirituality
Spirituality	Midrash Fiction	Women's Interest
Global Spiritual	Monasticism	Worship
Perspectives		

Or phone, fax, mail or e-mail to: SKYLIGHT PATHS Publishing
Sunset Farm Offices, Route 4 • P.O. Box 237 • Woodstock, Vermont 05091
Tel: (802) 457-4000 • Fax: (802) 457-4004 • www.skylightpaths.com
Credit card orders: (800) 962-4544 (8:30AM–5:30PM ET Monday–Friday)
Generous discounts on quantity orders. SATISFACTION GUARANTEED. Prices subject to change.

Printed in the USA
CPSIA information can be obtained
at www.ICGtesting.com
JSHW060056150824
68134JS00032B/2751

9 781594 731525